Published in 2013 by The Rosen Publishing Group, Inc.
29 East 21st Street, New York, NY 10010

Photo Credits: **KEY** tc=top center; tr=top right; cl=center left; c=center; cr=center right; bl=bottom left; bc=bottom center; br=bottom right; bg=background

CBCD = Corbis PhotoDisc; CBT = Corbis; GI = Getty Images; iS = istockphoto.com; N = NASA; SH = Shutterstock; TF = Topfoto

front cover bg SH; **back cover** cl N; **2–3**bg GI; **6**cl GI; **6–7**bg CBCD; **7**bc GI; **8–9**bg GI; **9**tr N; **10**bg, tl iS; **11**tr iS; **12**br, cl iS; **12–13**bg iS; **3**cl, cr, tr CBT; tl TF; **16**bg, cr iS; cl SH; **19**bg iS; **20**bg iS; bl, cr SH; **21**bg, cl, cr iS; bl SH; **22**bc CBT; c iS; cr SH; **22–23**bg, bg iS; **23**tr iS; br, c SH; **24**bl TF; **27**tr GI; **28**br iS; bl, tr CBCD; **29**tc CBT; bl iS; tr iS; bc TF; **30–31**bg CBCD.

All illustrations copyright Weldon Owen Pty Ltd. **24–25, 31**br Lionel Portier

Weldon Owen Pty Ltd
Managing Director: Kay Scarlett
Creative Director: Sue Burk
Publisher: Helen Bateman
Senior Vice President, International Sales: Stuart Laurence
Vice President Sales North America: Ellen Towell
Administration Manager, International Sales: Kristine Ravn

Library of Congress Cataloging-in-Publication Data
McFadzean, Lesley.
 Earth in peril / by Lesley McFadzean. —— 1st ed.
      p. cm. —— (Discovery education: the environment)
 Includes index.
 ISBN 978-1-4488-7889-5 (library binding) —— ISBN 978-1-4488-7977-9 (pbk.) ——
ISBN 978-1-4488-7983-0 (6-pack)
1. Environmentalism—Juvenile literature. 2. Environmental degradation—Juvenile literature.
I. Title.
 GE195.5.M45 2013
 304.2'8—dc23
                                        2011048218

Manufactured in the United States of America

CPSIA Compliance Information: Batch #SW12PK: For Further Information contact Rosen Publishing, New York, New York at 1-800-237-9932

EARTH IN PERIL

LESLEY MCFADZEAN

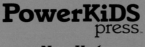

New York

Contents

Global Changes 6

Greenhouse Effect..................................8

Fossil Fuels 10

Acid Rain 11

Coasts Under Threat 12

Deforestation 14

Extreme Weather 16

Alternative Energy 20

You Decide 22

Recycling Trash 24

Slowing Down Change.........................26

Fact File 28

Glossary..30

Index 32

Websites...32

Global Changes

Floods, droughts, hurricanes, typhoons, cyclones, torrential rains, and heat waves have affected people throughout human history. But global warming has increased the frequency and severity of these extreme weather events in many parts of the world.

Global warming has also resulted in melting ice sheets, rising sea levels, and increases in ocean temperatures. Warmer oceans have a significant impact on weather and climate patterns. Increased hurricane activity in North America has been linked to rising sea temperatures in the Atlantic Ocean.

NORTH AMERICA

SOUTH AMERICA

ATLANTIC OCEAN

PACIFIC OCEAN

Drilling an ice core

Ice core

CLIMATE RECORDS

Written weather records go back hundreds of years, but ice cores from 11,900 feet (3,625 m) deep provide a 750,000-year climate history. Tree rings tell us about weather patterns back to 9,000 years ago. Scientists are still debating how changes in the sunspot cycle affect Earth's climate.

Ice cores
Scientists analyze gas concentrations in air trapped in between ice layers.

Tree rings
Dendrochronology is the study and dating of tree rings.

Sunspots
Darker, cooler spots on the Sun's surface increase and decrease in number over a cycle of 11 years.

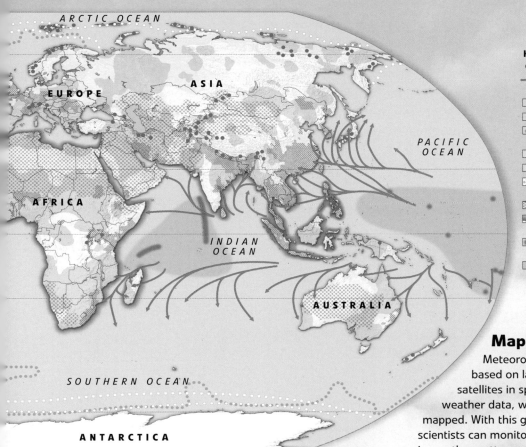

KEY
- ● Glacier
- ⟶ Typical hurricane tracks
- ▢ Winter ice extent
- ▢ Summer ice extent
- ▣ Extent of iceberg drifts
- ▢ Increase in drought
- ▢ Increased rainfall
- ⊠ Increase in mean temperature
- ▨ Flood hazard
- ◪ Coastal areas at greatest risk
- ▤ Islands and archipelagos at risk
- ▢ Areas of low-lying islands

Map of change

Meteorological stations based on land and satellites in space provide weather data, which can be mapped. With this global mapping, scientists can monitor any changes in weather patterns and assess the risks. They can then provide an early warning system.

Rising temperatures

By plotting the average global temperatures (red line on graph below) over the past 160 years, scientists can show that average temperatures have been rising steadily since the introduction of fossil fuels and engines.

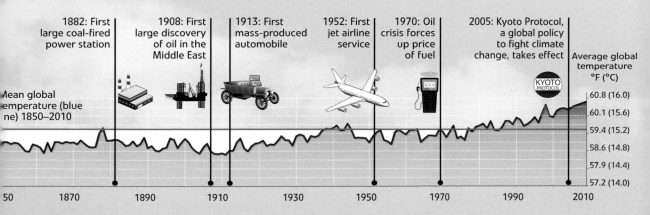

1882: First large coal-fired power station

1908: First large discovery of oil in the Middle East

1913: First mass-produced automobile

1952: First jet airline service

1970: Oil crisis forces up price of fuel

2005: Kyoto Protocol, a global policy to fight climate change, takes effect

KYOTO PROTOCOL

Average global temperature °F (°C)

Mean global temperature (blue line) 1850–2010

60.8 (16.0)
60.1 (15.6)
59.4 (15.2)
58.6 (14.8)
57.9 (14.4)
57.2 (14.0)

1850   1870   1890   1910   1930   1950   1970   1990   2010

Greenhouse Effect

S unlight streams through the window of a greenhouse and the
warmth it brings remains trapped inside the glass of the greenhouse.
There is a similar "greenhouse effect" on Earth but, instead of glass,
a layer of gases in the atmosphere traps the heat. These greenhouse
gases keep Earth warm enough for life to flourish on the planet.

However, factories, power stations, and transportation systems emit
additional greenhouse gases. Now, too much heat is being trapped
in the atmosphere, and the world is getting warmer.

GREENHOUSE GASES

Carbon dioxide (from burning fossil
fuels) and methane (from natural gas,
large trash heaps, and livestock gas)
make up 70 percent of the extra
greenhouse gases released by human
activities. Carbon dioxide can remain
in the atmosphere for up to 200 years.
The atmospheric lifetime of methane
is only 12 years.

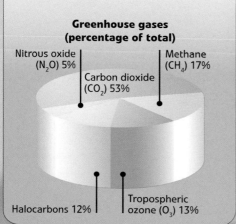

**Greenhouse gases
(percentage of total)**

Nitrous oxide
(N_2O) 5%

Methane
(CH_4) 17%

Carbon dioxide
(CO_2) 53%

Halocarbons 12%

Tropospheric
ozone (O_3) 13%

Reflected
Energy from
the Sun is
reflected into
the atmosphere.

Solar rays
Energy from
the Sun
reaches Earth.

Solar energy

Energy from the Sun passes through the atmosphere to Earth. Land and water absorb some and reflect the remainder back into the atmosphere (yellow arrows). However, much of the energy remains trapped (red arrows) by the extra greenhouse gases added to the atmosphere by human activity.

The Antarctic ozone hole
The purple area shows the thinning of the ozone layer in the stratosphere above Antarctica. Ozone absorbs ultraviolet light, so any thinning allows more ultraviolet light to reach Earth.

Ice mirror
Ice reflects more energy than other surfaces.

Trapped
Energy and heat are trapped by the greenhouse gas layer and reflected back to Earth.

That's Amazing!
It has been 115 years since the Swedish physicist Svante Arrhenius first warned the world that the burning of fossil fuels would eventually cause global warming.

Emitted
The heated land and seas release heat back into the atmosphere.

Fossil Fuels

Air travel
Aircraft release a lot of carbon dioxide high in the atmosphere, where it does the most damage. They also emit nitrogen oxides, which cause acid rain.

Coal, petroleum (oil), and natural gas are formed from fossilized organic material. That is why they are called "fossil fuels." Carbon-rich plant material, compressed for millennia by dense layers of rock above, forms coal. Oil and gas are formed, in a similar way, from the bodies of marine organisms.

When burned, the carbon in coal, oil, and gas is released into the atmosphere as carbon dioxide (CO_2).

CO_2 EMISSIONS
Tons (tonnes)
- 16.5+ (15+)
- 11–16.4 (10–14.9)
- 5.5–10.9 (5–9.9)
- 1.1–5.4 (1–4.9)
- Less than 1.1 (1)
- No data

NORTH AMERICA

EUROPE

ASIA

AFRICA

SOUTH AMERICA

AUSTRALIA

Fossil fuel emissions
This map shows that, on average, the most developed countries emit the most carbon dioxide. In the developing world, for example in China and in South America, emissions per person are lower but increasing fastest.

Peat
From recent plant deposits; has little carbon

Coal formation
In the Carboniferous period, 360–290 million years ago, vast amounts of land-based plants were deposited in shallow waters. This formed much of Earth's coal.

Lignite
Compacted by rock above; still 45 percent water

Black coal
Holds tar; used to produce coke for steel making

Anthracite
Buried longest; contains up to 95 percent carbon

Acid Rain

S ulfur oxides and nitrogen oxides cause acid rain, along with acid fog, acid snow, and acid hail. Air that has been polluted with these gases in one country can be blown thousands of miles (km) to fall as acid rain in another, possibly less polluted, country.

The level of acidity is measured on the pH scale—the lower the pH, the higher the acidity. Rain that has a pH of less than 5.5 is acid rain.

Killing forests
Acid rain can have devastating impacts on forests. The acid leaches vital minerals from the soil and from the trees' leaves. Without the minerals, the trees become weak and often die.

Creating acid rain
Nitrogen oxides are produced by the burning of fossil fuels in power stations, automobiles, factories, and homes. Sulfur oxides come from erupting volcanoes and the burning of some fossil fuels. When these gases react with water vapor in the atmosphere, they form acid rain.

Nitrogen oxides from car exhausts

Sulfur oxides from volcanic eruptions

Both oxides from coal-fired power stations

Acid gases in clouds produce acid rain.

Acid rain weakens and kills trees.

Acid rain pollutes ground water.

Coasts Under Threat

Low-lying coastal areas have always been prone to flooding when high tides and bad weather occur at the same time. Strong onshore winds, caused by approaching hurricanes, result in storm surges and a much higher storm tide than the usual high tides.

Scientists now believe that rising sea levels and an increase in extreme weather events, such as hurricanes, will affect coastal areas that have not been affected by floods before. They will also cause even greater devastation in coastal areas that are already prone to flooding.

If sea levels rise
Many coastal areas and major cities around the world are predicted to be at risk if sea levels continue to rise.

KEY
- Major cities at risk
- Coastal areas

1 Venice
Venice floods about four times a year when the tide rises more than 43 inches (110 cm). A new flood barrier system, due for completion in 2014, may not be able to protect Venice from future flooding, which some scientists believe could occur up to 250 times a year.

2 The Netherlands
The Netherlands is one of the so-called Low Countries, and a third of the country is below sea level. For thousands of years, the Dutch have built barriers and storm-surge dikes. This manipulated photo shows how the expected rise of the North Sea will overrun these dikes.

3 Bangladesh

Between 30 and 70 percent of Bangladesh's land floods every year. A recent report predicts that rising sea levels, a temperature increase of 2.5°F (1.4°C) by 2050, higher monsoon rainfall, and more cyclone activity will make the future for 147 million Bangladeshis much worse.

4 The Philippines

Coastal villagers in the Philippines build their houses on stilts in an attempt to escape floods. However, these stilts are not very strong and often collapse during the storm surges that accompany the increasingly frequent cyclones in the region.

5 Tuvalu

The 11,000 citizens of the nine islands of Tuvalu in the Pacific Ocean are looking for a new home. Sea levels rose 8–12 inches (20–30 cm) during the twentieth century and are still rising. Salt water has affected Tuvalu's water supply and food production.

6 Shishmaref

Inuit have lived on the island of Shishmaref, off Alaska, for 2,000 years, but they will soon relocate to the mainland. Rising temperatures have melted the permafrost on which the village is built, as well as the sea ice that used to protect the island from storm surges.

Deforestation

The world's forests help to maintain the balance of gases in the atmosphere. Trees take in carbon dioxide from the air and use it for photosynthesis. That is why forests are called carbon sinks—they drain carbon from the atmosphere. Trees release oxygen and water vapor back into the atmosphere, cleaning the air and providing the water vapor needed for rain clouds.

When forests are cleared, water vapor and oxygen are no longer released, and topsoil may blow away. Also, if trees or tree stumps are burned to clear land, they release huge quantities of carbon into the air.

That's Amazing!
The Amazon rain forest creates half of the rain that falls on it. Just 1 acre (0.4 ha) of tall canopy trees can release 20,000 gallons (76,000 l) of water a year.

Clouds fill with rain.

Trees release water vapor.

River releases water vapor.

Healthy forest
Although a small patch has been cleared, there are enough trees left to maintain the water cycle. The remaining trees still take in carbon dioxide from the atmosphere and release water vapor to produce rain.

No water vapor from cleared area

River silts up with soil.

Felled forest
There are too few trees left to release enough water vapor for rain. There are no tree roots to prevent soil runoff, so the river is clogged with soil. Without tree litter to provide nutrients, the soil becomes poor and crops fail.

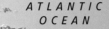

WORLD FORESTS
- Present forest extent
- Original forest extent

One-quarter of the world's forests lost in the past 10,000 years have been destroyed in the past 30 years.

Global deforestation

Almost half of the world's forests have disappeared during the past 2,000 years. At first, most forests were cleared by loggers or farmers. Now, land is cleared for houses, roads, railway lines, power stations, and power lines.

Less water vapor and less rain

AMAZON RAIN FOREST

The Amazon rain forest is the largest area of tropical rain forest in the world. About 60 percent of it is located in Brazil. Because of its size, the Amazon rain forest absorbs a significant proportion of the carbon dioxide created by human activities. Its deforestation will therefore contribute to global warming.

VEGETATION
- Tropical rain forest
- Deforested areas
- Other vegetation

Amazon River

B R A Z I L

Extreme Weather

Climate change has affected weather patterns and increased the frequency and the ferocity of extreme weather events. Hurricanes, cyclones, and typhoons are expected to be more frequent and more powerful in parts of the world. Heat waves, droughts, and wildfires will be more common. Precipitation—falling rain or snow—will increase elsewhere. Rising sea levels, combined with more powerful winds, will result in more storm surges and floods.

Heat waves

The Intergovernmental Panel on Climate Change predicts heat waves will become more common, especially in Europe and Asia. The number of extremely hot days in Europe has tripled since 1880. Heat waves last twice as long now as 130 years ago.

Recent heat waves
During the US heat waves in July and August 2008 and July 2009, 118-year-old temperature records were broken. In Europe in 2003, 35,000 people died from dehydration, heat exhaustion, heat stroke, and other heat-related illnesses.

Urban heat island effect
During heat waves, city temperatures can be 3.6–9°F (2–5°C) higher than in nearby rural areas. There are fewer trees to provide shade and release moisture, while sidewalks, roads, and buildings absorb and retain more heat.

Heat from the exhaust of buses, trucks, and automobiles adds to the urban heat island effect in cities.

Snow and ice storms

If the world is warming, why do we have snow and ice storms? In the longer term, as temperatures increase, there possibly will be less snow and ice. But for now, increases in storm activity and precipitation at 32°F (0°C) or below result in snow storms.

Snowflake crystals

Snowflakes

Precipitation is the moisture in clouds falling from the sky, usually as rain. Water freezes at 32°F (0°C). At that temperature, frozen ice crystals fall from clouds and create snowflakes. One drop of rain looks much like any other drop, but each snowflake is different.

Heading north

Snow storms have moved farther north in the US during the past 50 years. They are less frequent now but more severe, as seen in the "snowpocalypse" that hit the United States in February 2010.

AVALANCHE

An avalanche is like a landslide, but instead of rocks and mud, snow slides down the mountain. The farther it slides, the harder and faster it hits. Major temperature increases, strong winds, or human activity can cause avalanches.

New snow piles on wet snow.

The unstable surface slips.

Rescuers look for survivors.

Fresh snowfall

Surface avalanche

Avalanche buries village

Floods

There are three kinds of floods: coastal floods associated with storm surges; river floods, when heavy rain bursts riverbanks; and flash floods, when water races down canyons. More people die in floods than in any other natural disaster.

Italian flood
In October 2000, in the inland mountainous regions of northwest Italy, up to 28 inches (700 mm) of rain fell in six days. The rivers overflowed and flooded homes, and 20,000 people had to be evacuated.

Causes of drought
Drought is caused by less rain, combined with high temperatures that evaporate the rain on the ground. If rain does not fall at the right time of year, the result is also drought.

Drought

Drought is a long period with less rainfall than usual, which causes crops to fail. Drought is neither random nor rare in many regions of the world but, since the early 1970s, the percentage of drought-affected land has doubled.

EL NIÑO

El Niño is an unusual warming of the waters of the Pacific Ocean near the equator. El Niño occurs every two to seven years and affects weather patterns in the tropical regions of both hemispheres. The recent increase in the frequency and intensity of El Niño may be due to global warming.

Rain in western Pacific

Trade winds blow warm water west.

Cold water rises to surface.

Normal conditions
In normal years, warm surface waters, blown by trade winds from western South America to the western Pacific, bring rain to the western Pacific.

Torrential rain in South America

Winds change direction.

Cold water does not rise to surface.

El Niño conditions
In El Niño years, trade winds reverse direction. Torrential rain hits South America, and drought occurs in the western Pacific.

Alternative Energy

There are alternative ways of producing energy that emit no greenhouse gases, unlike energy from burning fossil fuels. Many of these alternatives use the renewable resources of sunlight, water, tides, wind, and underground steam to produce energy. It is also possible to create energy by splitting atoms or burning gas from garbage.

Faced with a constant demand for energy and an awareness of global warming, many countries are turning to these nonpolluting energy sources.

Wind power

The blades of these wind turbines turn in the wind. They look like airplane propellers but act like windmills. A drive shaft is connected to the rotating blades. It operates a generator that produces electricity.

Solar power

In US solar power plants or solar farms, thermal collectors focus heat to produce steam that powers a generator. In other parts of the world, arrays of solar or photovoltaic cells convert sunlight directly into electricity.

Tidal power

Underwater turbines operate like wind turbines but use the movements of tides and currents to turn the blades on the turbines and generate electricity. Water is much denser than wind, so tidal turbines and blades must be much stronger.

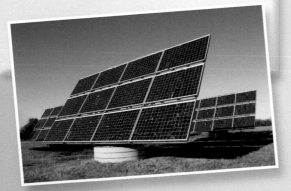

> " *The country that harnesses the power of clean, renewable energy will lead the 21st century.* "
> **US PRESIDENT BARACK OBAMA**

Hydroelectric power

The water of a fast-flowing river or waterfall flows through a pipe, called a penstock, and turns blades in a turbine. Increasingly, manmade dams that hold back water, then release it, are used in hydroelectric generation.

Nuclear power

When atoms are split into smaller particles, in a process called nuclear fission, they create energy or heat. Using uranium as a fuel, nuclear fission, carried out inside the reactor of a nuclear power plant, creates steam to generate electricity.

The world's first hydroelectric power plant was built almost 130 years ago at a dam on the Fox River in Wisconsin.

Geothermal power

Geothermal power harnesses energy from the Earth's interior to heat buildings or generate electricity. Most geothermal activity occurs at the boundaries between tectonic plates, where earthquakes and volcanoes occur.

Garbage power

When garbage buried in landfills decays, it releases methane gas (yellow arrows below). Deep down in all the garbage, the methane gas is collected and piped to a generator, where it is burned to produce electricity.

Generator

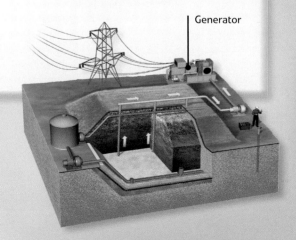

?... You Decide

Alternative energy sources do not emit greenhouse gases. Most are also sustainable and renewable. Fossil fuels emit greenhouse gases, take millions of years to form, and will run out some day. What would you like your country to do to satisfy energy demands in the future? You decide.

Petroleum
Crude oil is a yellow-black liquid found in reservoirs underground. It is used to generate electricity and as transportation fuel. Most countries import some or all of the oil they need and supplies are slowly running out.

Fossil fuels
Global demand for energy and transportation fuel is very high and increasing. We have come to depend on fossil fuels, and also have the knowledge and equipment to extract them from the ground. But they are harming our planet and will not last forever.

Coal
Coal is the oldest fossil fuel used by man to produce energy. Burning it emits four greenhouse gases. "Clean" coal reduces some of these emissions, but does not eliminate them.

Alternative energy

At present, only 7 percent of US energy comes from renewable resources. Alternative energy is more expensive to produce and the technology is still being developed. It may be some time before this percentage increases significantly. What is the solution?

Wind power

Energy from wind power has grown rapidly in recent years. In the United States, it provides electricity for 4.6 million homes. The wind turbine sites need careful selection as the wind must blow on the turbines almost constantly.

Nuclear power

Nuclear power can generate large quantities of electricity and does not emit greenhouse gases. Problems include safe disposal of nuclear waste, nuclear accidents, and nonrenewable uranium.

Natural gas

When burned, natural gas emits less carbon, sulfur, and nitrogen than other fossil fuels, but it still emits carbon dioxide. Its main ingredient is methane, also a greenhouse gas.

Solar power

Solar power is a sustainable, renewable resource but the amount of sunlight that reaches any given place is not constant. To trap the necessary amount of sunlight, you need large arrays of solar cells or thermal collectors.

Recycling Trash

Recycling is the third of the three Rs: reduce, reuse, recycle. Reduce the amount of plastic, glass, paper, and cans that you use. Reuse these things around your home. Only then, recycle them.

Throwing recyclable material in the trash creates mountains of garbage, which has to be burned in a process that releases carbon dioxide into the atmosphere. Alternatively, the garbage has to be buried in landfills, which release methane.

RECYCLING GLASS

Glass is an ideal material to recycle because it can be recycled and reused again and again. For every 1 ton (1 t) of glass that is recycled and made into a new product, 495 pounds (225 kg) of carbon dioxide is not emitted into the atmosphere.

This man sorts different types of glass at a recycling plant in New York.

The journey of a plastic bottle

Plastic is not organic so it does not break down—ever. Plastic bottles, particularly those used for bottled water, are a major problem for the environment and are increasing in number. Here are two ways we can deal with them.

OPTION 1

This is one of 29 billion plastic bottles bought in the United States each year.

OPTION 2

Trash can
In the developed world, 4 to 6 pounds (2–3 kg) of trash per person is dumped in trash cans each day. Two thirds of plastic bottles are sent to landfills instead of being recycled.

Landfills
Large areas of precious land have now become huge, smelly landfill sites, which are expensive to maintain. If people stop putting plastic bottles in the trash, the amount of landfill can be reduced.

Decomposition
A plastic bottle takes about 450 years to decompose.

Collection
Many areas have regular curbside collections of plastic bottles. If not, the bottles can be taken to plastic bottle banks or to drop-off centers.

Recycling container
Plastic bottles have a number in a triangle on the bottom. Bottles with the numbers 1 (PET) and 2 (HDPE) can be recycled.

Separation
At a material reclamation center, the plastic bottles are sorted according to type. Recyclable PET and HDPE bottles are separated from each other and from nonrecyclable PVC bottles.

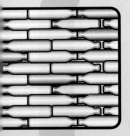

Squashed blocks
The sorted plastic bottles are squashed into solid blocks. The blocks are easier to handle and take up less space when they are transported in trucks.

New product
The clean flakes go to factories where recycled plastic products are made. The flakes are melted down and remolded into new plastic products.

Reprocessing
In the reprocessing factory, workers cut the blocks into small flakes. First, the flakes are washed to remove any dirt, grease, and labels, then they are dried.

Slowing Down Change

Of all the carbon dioxide emitted by human activities, 41 percent comes from industry (factories and power stations), 22 percent from transportation, and 33 percent from our homes—that is one third of all emissions. Homes built and equipped to minimize energy use also minimize greenhouse gas emissions.

Now there are many architects, builders, and kit-home suppliers specializing in eco-houses that minimize energy use. So-called "passive" houses are built using special materials, insulation, and heating technology so they use almost no energy for heating.

Eco-house

An eco-house minimizes the consumption of energy and water. Treating, pumping, and distributing water uses energy. Saving and recycling water can conserve energy and reduce a home's carbon footprint.

Double glazing
Double-glazed windows keep in heat during winter.

Drying clothes
Drying in the wind and sunlight, rather than a drier, uses zero energy.

Composting
Grass clippings, vegetable peelings, and eggshells can be composted.

Gray water pipes
Piping water from shower and sink drains to garden faucets reduces municipal water usage.

Recycling
Recyclables are separated from trash to minimize methane emitted from landfills.

Family transportation
A bicycle emits no greenhouse gases and an electric or hybrid automobile emits very little.

Rainwater tank
Collecting rainwater for use on the garden reduces municipal water use.

Appliances on standby mode contribute 5 percent of a home's total greenhouse gas emissions.

HOW SOLAR PANELS WORK

Solar or photovoltaic cells, made of silicon, produce an electrical current when exposed to sunlight. The technology was first used on the Sputnik 3 satellite in the 1950s. Now, arrays of photovoltaic cells in solar panels provide electricity and (water) heating for homes.

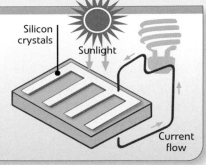

Silicon crystals

Sunlight

Current flow

Solar panels
These can be used to heat water and to generate electricity.

Wind turbine
When the rotor spins, it generates renewable energy.

Sun tube
This directs sunlight into a room to provide a source of natural light.

Insulation
Roof insulation retains heat in the home in winter.

Bathroom
A low-flow showerhead and low-flush toilet save water.

Ceiling fan
This uses 100 watts of electricity, while an air conditioner uses 7,500 watts.

Appliances
Energy-efficient electrical appliances reduce a home's carbon footprint.

Greenhouse
Heat is trapped and used to heat water.

Under-floor heating
Piped solar-heated water heats the house.

Washing clothes
Using a front loader and cold water is eco-friendly.

Gray water
Captured water from showers and sinks can be reused elsewhere.

Fact File

Weather is the temperature and precipitation on a particular day in a particular place. Climate is the average weather pattern over many years. To measure changes in the world's climate, scientists need very accurate data on weather going back as far as possible. Since 1880, weather data—first from land-based meteorological sites and now from satellites, too—has been coordinated globally.

STORMY WEATHER

2 **Greatest number thunderstorm days**
Average 322 days per year
Bogor, West Java, Indonesia

3 **Most lightning**
409 strikes per square mile per annum (158/km^2/yr)
Near Kifuka, Democratic Republic of Congo

4 **Heaviest hailstone**
2.25 pounds (1.02 kg)
April 14, 1986 Gopalganj, Bangladesh

5 **Largest hailstone**
18.75 inches (47.62 cm) in circumference
June 22, 2003 Aurora, Nebraska

That's Amazing!

The Central England Temperature record has kept monthly temperatures since 1659 and daily temperatures since 1772. It is the world's longest instrumental record of temperatures.

WIND SPEED

1 **Highest surface wind speed**
231 miles per hour (372 km/h)
Mt. Washington Observatory in New Hampshire

Lowest rainfall
Much of the Atacama Desert is in the Andes mountains. Not only is it the place with the lowest rainfall in the world, it is also cold compared with other deserts.

Most rainfall
The small village of Mawsynram took over the record as the wettest place in the world from nearby Cherrapunji. Most of the torrential rain in this area falls in the monsoon season, from April to October.

PRECIPITATION

9 **Highest annual average rainfall**
467.3 inches (11,849 mm)
Mawsynram, Meghalaya, India

10 **Highest 24-hour precipitation**
71.85 inches (1,825 mm) January 7–8, 1966
Foc-Foc, La Réunion, Indian Ocean

11 **Lowest annual average rainfall**
Parts of Atacama Desert in Chile, South America, have received no rain in over 400 years.

12 **Greatest one–day snowfall**
76 inches (1,930 mm) April 14–15, 1921
Silver Lake, Colorado

TEMPERATURE

6 **Highest temperature**
136°F (57.8°C) September 13, 1922
Al Azizyah, Libya

7 **Lowest temperature**
−128.6°F (−89.2°C) July 21, 1983
Vostok Station, Antarctica

8 **Greatest one day temp change**
From 44°F (6.7°C) to −56°F (−49°C)
January 23–24, 1916
Browning, Montana

Lowest temperature
Built in 1957, Vostok Station is near the South Geomagnetic Pole at the center of the East Antarctic ice sheet. With the lowest recorded temperature on Earth, no wildlife lives here.

Glossary

acid rain (A-sud RAYN)
Rain that contains acids formed when sulfur and nitrogen oxides combine with water vapor in the atmosphere.

carbon dioxide
(KAHR-bun dy-OK-syd) An odorless gas formed from one carbon atom and two oxygen atoms.

carbon footprint
(KAR-bun FUHT-print) A measure of the negative impact that a person, home, or business has on the environment.

carbon sink (KAHR-bun SINK)
A natural or artificial reservoir that absorbs carbon dioxide from the atmosphere and stores it for a significant period.

chlorofluorocarbons (CFCs)
(klor-oh-flor-oh-KAHR-bunz) Compound gases that contain carbon, chlorine, fluorine, and hydrogen.

clean coal (KLEEN KOHL) Any of a number of technologies designed to reduce emissions and pollutants from burning coal.

dendrochronology
(den-droh-kruh-NAW-luh-gee) The science of tree-ring dating based on the color and width of the rings.

dike (DYK) A long wall or embankment built as a flood-control measure.

eco–house (EE-koh-hows)
A house that conserves energy and water, while reducing waste, pollution, and carbon emissions.

El Niño (EL NEE-nyoh) A flow of warm surface waters in the equatorial zone of the Pacific Ocean, off the western coast of South America.

flash flood (FLASH FLUD) A sudden, severe flood that rushes downhill to low-lying areas after heavy rain or the breaching of a dam on higher land.

fossil fuels (FO-sul FYOOLZ) Hydrocarbons formed from plant and animal remains compressed for millions of years under layers of rock.

geothermal power
(JEE-oh-ther-mul POW-er) Power generated from the heat stored deep in Earth's core.

global warming
(GLOH-bul WAWRM-ing) An increase in average temperatures of Earth's atmosphere, over an extended period of time, which causes changes in global climate.

greenhouse effect
(GREEN-hows eh-FEKT) The rise in Earth's temperature due to additional greenhouse gases emitted by human activities into the atmosphere.

greenhouse gas
(GREEN-hows GAS) One of a number of gases that absorbs and traps infrared radiation from the Sun.

hybrid automobile
(HY-brud AH-toh-moh-beel) An automobile that runs on two or more fuels, for example, an automobile with a gasoline engine and an electric motor.

methane (MEH-thayn) The simplest hydrocarbon, formed by the decomposition of organic matter in the absence of oxygen.

nitrogen oxides
(NY-truh-jen OK-sydz) Gases that contain varying amounts of nitrogen and oxygen, some of which are toxic.

nuclear fission
(NOO-klee-ur FIH-shun) The splitting of atoms to form smaller atoms and release energy.

organic (or-GA-nik)
Describes anything that comes from a once-living organism (plant or animal) and often contains carbon.

penstock (PEN-stawk) A pipe or tube that carries water from a river, reservoir, or dam to a turbine or water wheel.

permafrost (PUR-muh-frost) Ground, in areas near the South and North poles, that is permanently frozen down to the subsoil.

photovoltaic cell (foh-toh-vol-TAY-ik SEL) A cell that converts sunlight directly into electricity.

precipitation (preh-sih-pih-TAY-shun) Any form of water—rain, snow, hail, or sleet—falling to Earth from a cloud filled with water vapor.

renewable resource (ree-NOO-uh-bul REE-sawrs) A natural resource that continues to be replenished in a relatively short period of time.

soil runoff (SOY-ul RUN-of) Soil that is washed away by water, such as heavy rain or flood, which enters the nearest stream or river.

storm surge (STORM SERJ) An abnormal rise in sea level caused by the high onshore winds of a hurricane, cyclone or typhoon.

storm tide (STORM TYD) The abnormally high sea level that results from a high tide combined with a storm surge. It is sometimes called a hurricane tide.

sulfur oxides (SUL-fur OK-sydz) Gases emitted by the burning of fuels such as coal and oil that contain sulfur or by industrial processes such as smelting.

sustainable resource (suh-STAY-nuh-bel REE-sawrs) A natural resource that is used or harvested in a way that does not reduce the amount of the resource to a dangerously low level and does not permanently damage it.

thermal collector (THER-mul kuh-LEK-tur) A mirror or lens that collects energy from the Sun and then focuses it to heat water to a high enough temperature to create steam, which is then used to generate electricity.

turbine (TER-byn) A machine or engine with a set of rotating vanes, attached to a central spindle, which move or turn using the force of water, wind, or steam.

ultraviolet light (ul-truh-VY-uh-let LYT) A type of invisible, high-energy radiation with a shorter wavelength than visible light.

uranium (yoo-RAY-nee-um) A natural silvery metallic element, which is radioactive and highly toxic, and is used for nuclear power generation and in nuclear weapons.

Index

A
acid rain 11
alternative energy 20, 21, 23
avalanche 17

C
carbon dioxide 8, 10, 14, 15, 24, 26
carbon footprint 26, 27
climate 6, 28
    change 7, 16
    records 6
coal 7, 10, 11, 22
    clean 22
cyclones 6, 13, 16

D
deforestation 14, 15
drought 6, 16, 19

E
eco-house 26, 27
El Niño 19
extreme weather 6, 12, 16

F
flood 6, 12, 13, 16, 18
fossil fuels 8, 9, 10, 11, 20, 22

G
global warming 6, 9, 15, 19, 20
gray water 26, 27
greenhouse gases 8, 20, 22, 23, 26

H
heat wave 6, 16
hurricane 6, 12, 16

L
landfills 21, 24, 26

M
methane 8, 21, 23, 24, 26

N
natural gas 8, 10, 23
nuclear fission 21

O
ozone 8, 9

P
petroleum 10, 22
plastic 24, 25
precipitation 16, 17, 28

R
rainfall 13, 19, 28, 29
recycling 24, 25, 26

S
sea level 6, 12, 13, 16
snow 11, 16, 17
solar panel 27
solar power 20, 23
storm surges 12, 13, 16, 18

T
temperature 6, 7, 13, 16, 17, 19, 28, 29
thermal collector 20
tides 12, 20
turbine 20, 21, 23, 27

U
uranium 21, 23
urban heat island 16

W
wildfire 16
wind 12, 16, 17, 19, 20, 23, 26, 27, 28

Websites

Due to the changing nature of Internet links, PowerKids Press has developed an online list of websites related to the subject of this book. This site is updated regularly. Please use this link to access the list: www.powerkidslinks.com/disc/earth/